FOR LOVE
OF HOME

Barbara Kutner and Amy Obenhofer

AuthorHouse™
1663 Liberty Drive
Bloomington, IN 47403
www.authorhouse.com
Phone: 833-262-8899

Because of the dynamic nature of the Internet, any web addresses or links contained in this book may have changed since publication and may no longer be valid. The views expressed in this work are solely those of the author and do not necessarily reflect the views of the publisher, and the publisher hereby disclaims any responsibility for them.

Any people depicted in stock imagery provided by Getty Images are models, and such images are being used for illustrative purposes only.
Certain stock imagery © Getty Images.

This book is printed on acid-free paper.

ISBN: 979-8-8230-1420-5 (sc)
ISBN: 979-8-8230-1422-9 (hc)
ISBN: 979-8-8230-1421-2 (e)

Library of Congress Control Number: 2023917248

Print information available on the last page.

Published by AuthorHouse 11/30/2023

author HOUSE

CONTENTS

To Patti, with love,

from, Mom and Amy.

PREFACE

This is a book about the journey of three women who have a passion for making their homes reflect how they connect with one another. This is done by creating spaces that lend themselves to their creativity—spaces where they can experience the joy and satisfaction of a pleasing environment while having fun doing it. The three women are my mother, my sister, and myself. Three very different styles. It is not a how-to-decorate book that tells you about the placement of furniture or how high a picture should be hung. It's about instinct, passion, and creativity. As a matter of fact, all three of us would have liked to have had jobs where we could have used our creativity, styles, and taste. Instead, we are a retired headmistress, a banker, and a librarian. Not exactly the most creative fields in the world. No wonder we needed an outlet to share our inspirations.

Our book breaks down the relationship between our homes and our happiness. As an unknown author said, "A house is made with walls and beams. A home is made with love and dreams." Everyone knows that our homes are supposed to make us happy, and in turn, if we are happy, our home will be a happy place.

Looking past recent decorating trends and decorating for show, our homes tell a story about each of us. What do we love? What are we passionate about? Why does a flea market treasure excite us? How do our homes reflect our personalities? Our homes welcome family and friends to share in our joy and the items we love. Through this experience, we have become collectors of some of our most precious finds, and in doing so, we have become knowledgeable about our collections and decorating styles.

Patti was one of those people who graciously welcomed people into her beautiful home. She had taste, elegance, and style. She taught us about her decorating ideas and was an integral part of our three-way circle; always looking for treasures with us. She was there to remind us to buy what we loved. Don't buy something just because it's cheap—a habit we find hard to break. For all that she was to us, we want to dedicate this book to her, our daughter, sister, and friend who passed away on January 7, 2016.

Patti would be appalled to think that we were writing a book because she was a talented writer with a journalism degree, as well as a degree in library science, a perfectionist in all she did. And us, we just get it done.

INTRODUCING BARB

Can you imagine a ten-year-old girl getting excited about seeing tarnished sterling silver turn from an ugly black color to a gleaming shine as pieces were carefully polished? Can you imagine a ten-year-old girl thinking that her neighbor's flowered sofas were something she loved to look at, and she thought were exceptionally pretty? She later learned the fabric on these sofas was called chintz. This girl also admired oil paintings, old glass lamps with flowered shades, French doors, and wallpaper in beautiful prints. The girl is me!

Can you imagine a ten-year-old who loves sterling silver and chintz fabrics?

For whatever reason, I was always aware of my surroundings, and they were important to me. I've even been known to rearrange motel rooms to make them more functional and attractive. I might have to surmise that there is something in my genes that causes me to need to make my environment as pleasing as possible.

When I got married, this need caused considerable internal conflict for me. We had little money to furnish our first apartment, so I tried hard to make it to my liking. Not easy to do with my aunt's old brown frieze sofa, a used maple table and chairs, my mother-in-law's ugly bedroom set, and walls that were painted pea green. The apartment was so dark and dreary that I bought white, ruffled Cape Cod curtains to try to give it a colonial look, which only made everything else look even worse. I really did not like the way the apartment looked.

The Cape Cod curtains didn't work.

Our neighbors in the apartment across the hall had a different look than I had. It was Scandinavian in style with a modern sofa with clean lines and bright blue fabric streaked with silver threads. The end tables were blond wood, which was a style also popular in the 1950s. Even though everything in their apartment was brand-new and my things were old and mismatched, I still liked my apartment better. What was wrong with me?

After a year of living in what I thought was an awful place, we were able to buy our first house—a little three-bedroom ranch—and I was in my glory. The Cape Cod curtains went much better in this house, and my husband wallpapered the dinette and our bedroom in wonderful mini prints that made my heart race with joy. I was so excited to have the wallpaper of my dreams. He also painted the bathroom—three times until I got the color right!

We were able to buy a new sofa and a chair for the living room. I loved this beautiful house. Moreover, to make this house even more special, my husband decided to build a garage and a screened porch. I was a little concerned because he spent a great deal of time staring at the space where the garage was going to be, and I wondered what he was doing. I learned that my husband was thinking (imagine that) about how to build the garage, and I also learned that he was very talented with a hammer. I was so relieved because my father didn't know which end of a hammer to use. From then on, my husband and I were a team. He could do carpentry, wiring, plumbing, painting, and designing, and best of all, he had a wonderful aesthetic sense, so he didn't just build; he created beautiful spaces. As Patti said, "Dad can do anything," and she was right. Since then, we have renovated and decorated a series of homes during the sixty-five years we have been married. Every time we finished a project, I would get so excited about what we had accomplished that you would have thought we had won the lottery.

You must plan before building a garage.

When we purchased our second home, my style and taste began to take form, and my journey began. After trips to Williamsburg, Virginia, Sturbridge, Massachusetts, and living in Connecticut, I became interested in period furniture, oriental carpets, and artwork, none of which I could afford. However, I didn't let that stop me. Early attic began calling to me. On the weekends, while our husbands watched the children, my neighbors and I went to antique shows looking for bargains. We'd spend the next week refinishing and refurbishing our treasures. We called ourselves "the South Cross Strippers" because we lived on South Cross Trail.

While I was in the grocery store one time, I overheard two women talking, and one of them said, "Have you heard about the women who live on South Cross Trail? They call themselves the South Cross Strippers. What do you think that is all about?" I didn't bother to fill them in, but it gave me a good laugh.

My style has never changed. I still have many of the same pieces I acquired when we were first married, and I love them every bit as much now as I did then. When decorating my home, I try to incorporate good design with what I love. I think the attributes of a lovely home might include warmth, comfort, familiarity, eye appeal, quality materials on upholstered pieces, color, and a focal point in a room, such as a fireplace, a bank of windows, or a seating grouping. I ask myself, *Will an old piece do just as well as a new one? Does it make me happy?* I like to use the concepts of repetition and variation in my decorating. Some of the details have changed in my house as I've incorporated different items, depending on my mood, the season, or a new acquisition, but basically the style doesn't change. I try to make my home a place where comfort and beauty marry. It has been a wonderful journey that I have experienced with my daughters.

The bachelor chest I have had forever and still love.

Our Home.

INTRODUCING AMY

My mom loved antiques when I was growing up, and I remember thinking, *I will never have that old stuff in my house, just shiny, new things.*

The first time I can ever remember thinking or caring about decorating was when I was in college. I wanted my room to look nice, so I designed fabric wall hangings stretched on wooden frames that created a certain modern flair. They were bright orange and brown. (None of that old stuff.) I had a chrome side table, a brown bedspread, and a brown slingback sort of chair. It was my very own, and I loved it. While everyone else had typical dorm stuff, I had a more sophisticated, pulled-together look. Or so I thought. And so, it began.

My first job out of college was as an assistant buyer in a department store. I thought *this would be great. I will get to look at all the latest trends and be right in the thick of things in the fashion world.* Much to my dismay, I was placed as the assistant buyer in the bed and bath department. *Really? How am I going to wear towels?* Unbeknown to me, this would be the start of my home decor inspiration.

I worked long hours in retail and never really thought about decorating until I got my own apartment. I rented a one-bedroom apartment in an old Victorian house on Meigs Street in Rochester, New York. I had the original house's kitchen with tons of cupboards and the traditional yellow linoleum flooring. The charm was in the living area, where I had a quaint window seat in a bay window, tall ceilings, and large crown moldings. It was mine, and I was excited. The only problem was that I had no money. So, my home at the time consisted of leftovers from my mom's house and a floral love seat I bought. (I did like that love seat.) I made chintz curtains out of $1.99-a-yard fabric for the window seat area and covered the cushions in the same fabric. That was about the extent of my decorating of my first apartment.

I was married on August 26, 1989. The first home we bought was a 1910 1,565-square-foot colonial with three bedrooms and one bath. We borrowed money from my parents and my husband's sister to make a down payment. The home had beautiful gumwood trim, stained glass windows, and high ceilings. The kitchen was big with lots of old, cheap wooden cabinets and, of course, linoleum flooring. There was carpet in the dining and family room, which was separated by gumwood pillars. Upstairs we had yellow pine floors, which I loved. There was a tiny bathroom, a sleeping porch off one of the bedrooms, and a huge walk-up attic that had tons of storage. My husband and I worked tirelessly on restoring the home to its former glory—on a shoestring budget, of course. We ripped up the linoleum in the kitchen to find another layer of glued-on red and black tiles. I spent weeks on my hands and knees scraping black glue off the floor so that we could have it refinished. Under the massacre of layers were maple 1.5-inch-wide boards. After they were refinished, they were so beautiful, and they brightened the whole house. The kitchen cabinets were another story. What do you do when you are on a budget to make your cabinets look good? You paint them, and, of course, you don't hire anyone; you do it yourself. At the time, dark green was really in, so I painted all the cabinet doors dark green with a white base. Gorgeous, as you can imagine. As time went on, we worked on countless projects to restore the original beauty of the home. *Hmm, am I turning into my mother?* I thought.

I decorated that house in a country style the best I could. I bought a set of old oak T-back chairs with brown leather seats, and I refinished them (one of my first refinishing projects). I replaced the seats with red-and-green calico fabric, and I had a slipcover made for my husband's bachelor pad couch in dark green plaid. Are you getting the theme here? I bought an old wainscot cupboard at a flea market and had my husband cut out the back so we could put the TV in it. I really didn't want the ugly TV as part of my decorating theme. After all, I was creating a showcase.

When our first Christmas rolled around in this house, I went to town. I put greens on every inch of that house. I wrapped the pillars separating the dining and family room with red velvet ribbon. I had red and green bows on every bough, and I wrapped every Christmas package in brown wrapping paper with red and green plaid bows. I even made a holiday wreath that included turkey feathers, to appease my husband, who was a hunter. I had cinnamon-smelling pinecones in baskets and candles circled in garlands on every surface. There was no mistaking it was Christmas in that house. My sister called it "The Christmas House."

THE CHRISTMAS HOUSE

Ribbons

Red bows

Ever green boughs

Brown wrapping paper

Candles

Holly

Gifts

Not a single symbol was missing!

While living in this house, I worked for a bank. Yes, it is a long story. One of my friends at the bank told me about a flea market where I could buy things cheaper than at an antique show. I went to this flea market in Avon, New York, and thought I died and went to heaven. Wow, an outlet to buy things for my home. I would get up early Sunday morning before dawn, grab my flashlight and bag, and out the door I went. We diehards were there early to get a look at new merchandise coming off the freshly loaded trucks of "pickers" who had spent the week scouring garage and household sales for new treasures to sell to inquiring minds such as myself. The thrill of the hunt and the anticipation of finding a sleeper filled me with excitement. The market was bustling in the morning with other early birds and the smell of freshly made doughnuts and stale popcorn from the night-before moviegoers. The flea market was located at a drive-in movie theater. The air was stifling in the dead of summer and crisp in the late fall. I soon became a regular of this ritual, and I enjoyed my quiet alone time lost in deep thought and concentrating on finding a treasure.

At the time, I was really interested in primitive items—furniture and baskets with old paint and wooden items smoothed over by time and the touch of a hand. I often thought about who had used the items before me, how they used the items and what they would think now if they lived in my world. I learned how to speak the flea market lingo by asking things like, "What is your best price?" so as not to offend anyone. I learned that if I hesitated for too long, someone else would swoop in and purchase the item under my nose. This happened more than once. Life was good for a young professional on a tight budget, dying to make her home speak to the world in a spectacular show of style and class.

My primitive look.

My solitude was soon interrupted when I introduced my mother and sister to flea markets. The first time I brought my mom to the flea market in Avon, New York, she could not believe it. At that time, flea markets were filled with antiques—items from long ago, tossed aside to purchase shiny new items. It was unlike today, where you find an ample number of t-shirts, purses, dog bones, and more. Mom was dismayed at the inexpensive purchases she could make to fill her home as well.

My sister, on the other hand, was of the notion that if a treasure didn't cost a lot, it probably was not good. She had exquisite taste and wanted only the truest and finest antiques in her home. One time, we were at a flea market, and my sister asked how much something was, and the dealer promptly replied, "Seven dollars." My sister replied, "Seventy dollars?" and the dealer once again said, "Seven dollars." Clearly, my sister couldn't believe what she was hearing, and my mom and I finally said, "It's seven dollars. Buy it."

Decorating gives me a feeling of satisfaction, a sense of purpose. I feel complete after I finish a project and someone comments on how lovely it looks. Over the years, as you will learn, my style changed and evolved, depending on circumstances that affected my life. It's been a lifelong journey that I have shared with my mom and sister.

Living room in our present house.

The office gives me another space to display my ship picture collection.

A place to relax, enjoy my coffee, and watch the sun rise.

Our house today.

INTRODUCING PATTI

Patti was unique. She was very sure of herself and always knew what she wanted. She was extremely creative. When she was in grade school, in the summer, she was the one who thought up things for the neighborhood kids to do. Sometimes she would have a pet show or an art show. Of course, there were always prizes for every category imaginable.

The summer of *The Sound of Music* almost did in the whole neighborhood. Patti wrote the script for *The Sound of Music* and gathered all the kids and assigned them their parts. Then she painted the scenery on old bed sheets, and the mountains came alive as she hung them from clotheslines between trees in the backyard. In addition, she designed and made the costumes for each participant, so out the door went lace curtains, aprons, blouses, and whatever else she could find. For the wedding scene, she borrowed a wedding dress from one of the actors' mothers that had about fifty buttons on the back.

Moreover, Patti insisted that they practice every day, and she was no easy task master. Soon there was a bit of a rebellion against her idea, and she became terribly upset. I suggested she give the kids a little break, which to her credit she did, and soon, all was back on track. The wedding scene was a challenge because no sooner did the mother behind the scenes get all the buttons fastened on the wedding dress than she had to unfasten them in time for the next scene. The play was an enormous success. When Patti passed, her father and I received notes from neighborhood children who were in the play and remembered their part in the production. Oh, did I mention Patti wrote the play, designed the scenery, created the script, and starred in the role of Maria? Does that give you an idea of who Patti was?

Patti starring in the neighborhood production of *The Sound of Music*.

In grade school, Patti authored stories and poetry with illustrations. In high school, she took a home-decorating course, and her assignment was to create a model home and furnish it with a style she favored. Surprisingly, she implemented my style. Of course, she received an A for her grade. She spent hours in her bedroom and was happiest when she was working on an artistic project. She continued to learn and appreciate various forms of art, especially the famous painters of earlier periods, which she studied in college.

As a young bride, she and her husband moved to Tokyo for four and a half years, and Patti became knowledgeable about Japanese art and decorating. She liked simple lines, space around her artwork, and monochromatic color schemes. She would also rather do without than purchase something of lesser quality. Her apartment in Tokyo had many Japanese and Chinese items, which she purchased in shops in both countries. Her homes reflected the serene, calm Japanese nature that was so prevalent in Japan.

apartment in Tokyo

Patti and Andy's Tokyo apartment.

When she returned to the States, she enjoyed prowling through antique shops and joining us in our searches through flea markets and at house sales and consignment shops. Her style never changed. She was a minimalist but created warm, inviting spaces through her love of art, her use of subdued color, and her wonderful sense of design and style. She and her husband had a beautiful home in Bronxville, New York, and later purchased a lake house on Canandaigua Lake in Canandaigua, New York, which she decorated in her special style. In this house, she decorated it with blue instead of the beige and black she used in her other homes. It reflected the water and sky that were so much a part of her lake home. Although Patti's journey was short, we learned much from her, and she will always be a part of our three-way circle.

Lake house dining room and kitchen.

Lake house living room.

Patti and Andy's Lake house.

BARB'S RESOURCES FOR DECORATING

You can furnish your home by calling an interior decorator who will help you choose furnishings that will be perfectly matched and make your house look lovely. Another option is to go to a furniture store, and in one shopping spree, you can buy everything for your home. Furnishings will be new, stylish, and coordinated—or you can do it the *hard way*, by yourself. I don't see this as the hard way but as the fun way! Thrift shops, consignment shops, house sales, antique shops, and flea markets are all fun places to look for treasurers to furnish a home.

Linen chairs purchased at a house sale and recovered

Thrift shop, consignment shops and house sale purchases

We spend a lot of time in consignment shops, which are wonderful places to find gently used furniture, rugs, paintings, dishes, and other furnishings for your home. The beauty of a consignment shop purchase is that it is usually of better quality and more affordable than buying something new. We bought light fixtures, rugs, artwork, dishes, mirrors, and all manner of items at a consignment shop. Another advantage of visiting consignment shops is that you can also sell things there. For instance, if you purchased a table at the shop, and a few years later, you see one you like better, you can sell the original table there and then purchase the new one.

House sales have plentiful bargains, and all three of us have made purchases at them. For instance, I have an oriental rug and a pair of matching side chairs that are in my living room. I recovered them in a beautiful screen-printed, linen fabric. House sales are also great places to find artwork.

Just Google consignment shops, thrift shops, or house sales in your area, and you will find many to choose from near your home. All these places have been a part of our decorating journey. Whenever we look around at the items in our homes, they tell the story of the adventures and the fun times we had together shopping in these unique shops for treasurers.

Table purchased at an antique shop and refinished by the South Cross Stripper.

Ginger jars purchased at an antique shop

Restore opportunities

In our area, we have a Restore run by Habitat for Humanity where folks donate unwanted goods to charity, and the store resells the items for a profit. This is an especially wonderful place to find good-quality used items. Again, they have everything imaginable for the home. At holiday time, you can find decorations at very reasonable prices, and I see people doing holiday shopping. My granddaughter, Grace, found a perfect lamp for her new apartment. It is amazing the wonderful items you can find in these stores.

Grace's restore purchase.

Tavern table found at an antique mall.

Blue and white lamp found in a restore.

Fifty-dollar flea market chandelier.

CHILDREN'S ARTWORK AS A SOURCE FOR DECORATING YOUR HOME

Need some artwork for your walls, but your budget is tight? How about framing some of your children's or your artwork? Amy's children were two years apart in school, but they both had the same art teacher in high school and were assigned to paint a watercolor still life of a vase of flowers. They were not artists in any sense, but the pictures were lovely, and Amy had them framed. They were a perfect addition to her home. Of course, one of them got a better grade than the other, so that was always a bone of contention between them.

When Grace was young, she would make pen and ink drawings and put prices on them to sell at an antique shop where Amy had a booth in an antique co-op. I framed two of them and have them hanging in my laundry room. They are whimsical and fun, and only cost me fifty cents apiece, plus frames.

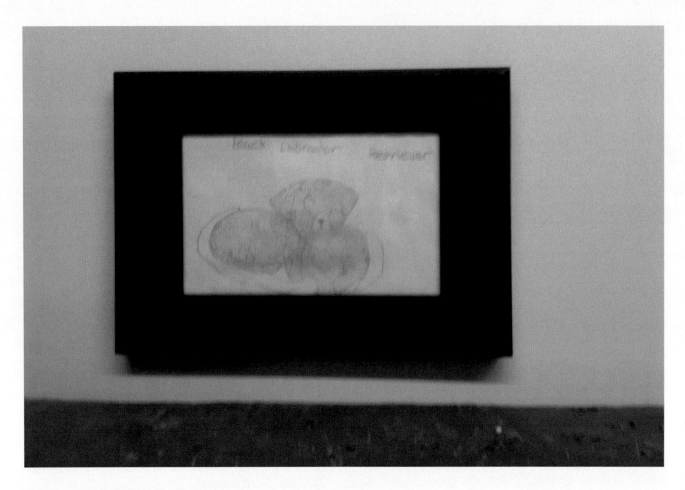

A friend framed artwork done by children in her elementary classroom and hung them in her back hall. Everyone stops to admire them as they enter her house. They make a unique and creative statement.

Children's artwork can be a fun and personal way of adding interest to your decorating.

ARTWORK ENHANCES OUR HOMES

Painting by Waddie Pipper, author of *The Little Engine That Could*, from Patti's artwork collection.

The seagull was purchased at an outdoor antique show one summer by Patti.

An oil painting of the Scottish Highlands over my mantel.

Amy's chickens
As Patti taught us, buy what you love, and that is what Amy did
when she purchased this piece of artwork; she has it hanging in her
family room, and it always brings a smile to people's faces.

Amy's clam shell painting complements the shades of blue in her living room and adds an element of fun to the room.

A HOBBY AS A SOURCE OF DECORATING

I became interested in rug hooking as another source of decorating my home. I made runners, rugs, wall hangings, and eventually branched into using this hobby for gifts. I made and framed rug-hooked pictures of Santa as well as rug-hooked Christmas pillows as gifts. I have several friends who turned this hobby into a business, selling their projects and doing custom work for friends, using their skill and creativity to earn income. You never know when a hobby might turn into a business or a decorating opportunity. Grace hangs the Santa I gave her in her home at Christmastime.

Santa finds a home as a Christmas gift.

A story rug hooked by me depicting years of family
vacations, given as gifts to my daughters.

SEASONAL DECORATING

Sometimes I just want to change the look of my rooms, and seasonal decorating is a great way to do this. Often I just move the furniture around, but another option is to use different accessories, which can give your house a completely changed feeling. Scout around your house for an interesting basket, bowl, vase, or other objects that would make a suitable container for an arrangement you might want to make using garden flowers, greens, berries, leaves, vegetables, or fruit. Select colors that complement your house, or maybe use something quite out of the ordinary. Have fun creating a new focal point for your room. You will be surprised by how adding a simple arrangement or moving things around, you can change the appearance and feel of your home. When Amy married Mark, and before he understood her decorating compulsion, he would be confused when he got home from work, because very often everything had changed when he came in the door. Now he gets it. Some examples of things we have tried follow:

Use candles to reflect the season and change the look.

Flowers can easily add color and cheer to a room.

Amy changes the contents of these pots with the seasons.

I change this bowl with different seasonal materials on a regular basis.

Simple elegance.

FLEA MARKETS

Over the years, we continued our interest in decorating. Each of us has our own style, and we have fun looking for things for one another's homes. We were so excited when Amy introduced us to flea markets, where we could find treasures that were a lot less expensive than in the antique shops. Besides visiting local markets, we also went to a huge flea market in Madison Bouckville, New York and one in Brimfield, Massachusetts, looking for that perfect item as we walked for hours in the hot sun or pouring rain. We were hooked. It's almost like we had a disease that kept calling to us to look for more bargains. We had two rules as we shopped together. Rule number one was whoever saw an item first had their first chance at it, and rule number two was if you wanted something, you had better buy it, because we probably would not go back since the place was so big.

Flea markets are amazing places. You can find just about anything imaginable for sale in all kinds of conditions, from nearly perfect to something badly in need of loving care. The dealers arrive at four in the morning to set up their booths in huge, open fields and along the streets. They usually have covers over their wares to protect them from the weather but not always.

Sometimes you see someone with items just set up on a table. Many dealers specialize in items, such as China, glassware, books, primitives, vintage, artwork, furniture, baskets, plants, or food, and some have a bit of everything. It can be overwhelming the first time you go. Vendors develop a reputation and are known for high prices but good quality, others for low prices and perhaps poor quality and anywhere in between.

As Amy taught us, there is an art to purchasing items at a flea market. We learned that prices can be negotiated, but you need to know the right way to approach a dealer. You must be careful not to offend the dealer, and you need to be able to walk away on good terms should you decide not to make the purchase. We all learned this the hard way. The best way to negotiate with a dealer is to ask him/her, "Is this your best price?" Then you can decide what you want to offer or how to proceed from there. Another option is called bundling, where you offer to buy several pieces in a booth for a negotiated price. This method can work well for both the dealer and the buyer.

For many years, while living in Connecticut, the Elephant Trunk Flea Market in New Milford, Connecticut, was a weekly stop for us. At the time, it was an unknown gem.

Now, however, it is featured on the TV show *Flea Market Flip*, making it harder to find real treasurers. Over the years, I found a set of Nantucket baskets, pewter pieces, furniture, and rugs that I still love. Our grandson, Connor, Amy's son, was born in October, and shortly after his birth, Amy, Connor, my husband, and I went to the Elephant Trunk Flea Market on a pretty cold morning. As Amy was walking around with Connor bundled up in his carrier, a woman walked by and in no uncertain terms told Amy that baby Connor did not belong there on such a cold morning. The lady was probably right, but she didn't understand what it is like to have the flea market bug.

As we approached each market, we got so excited, anticipating what we might find on that day's visit. There were many things we had no interest in, but when we spotted that one special prize, it made our day.

THE CUPBOARD

Steamy does not begin to describe the day. Oppressive, with a little sprinkle of excitement and perspiration are more like it. Mom, my sister, and I were headed to the Madison Bouckville, New York Antique Flea Market. It was 6:00 a.m., and with water bottles, hats, and carts in tow, we set out for an adventure. More than two thousand dealers peddle their wares. We all had delusions of grandeur that we would find the perfect item for our homes. The anticipation of finding a sleeper loomed large, and it was every woman for herself, even among relatives. It was a smorgasbord of everything old, odd, and original, and we were drooling at the opportunity to participate.

Picture a cow pasture with greasy food vendors, porta potties, and golf carts, and you pretty much get the picture. Add to that the steamy heat, and, well, you get the idea. I had partaken in this venue before, but Mom and my sister were new to this field of dreams. They were used to me moving quickly down the aisles in fear I might miss something. They strolled behind me, carefully inspecting items, while I continued my march onward. My sister was overjoyed by only the finest antiques, while my mom looked for the best buys, and I was all about primitive painted antiques. We all had very different styles and tastes, but the passion for what we were doing was clear. None of us needed anything, but whoever does? It is all about want. It was a bond that tied us together. It made us feel supported and close, and everything else in the world at that very moment didn't exist. Though don't get me wrong—we were still highly competitive with our finds. If two of us spotted an item at the same time, we had to have a discussion around who saw it first and whose house it would go into. This usually took place between my mom and me because my sister was out of our price range with her purchases. Mom usually relented because she was always putting others ahead of herself.

A quick break to consume a hot dog and lemonade would give us enough energy to keep going. We finished the majority of all two thousand booths and were rounding the corner to end our journey with dirt-stained legs and faces, and there it was. The mother of all cupboards. It was big. My adrenaline started to kick in, and I could feel my energy rise, but I had to play it cool. What was the price of this beauty? (My husband, brother-in-law, and father would beg to differ.) Was there anyone else looking at it? How eager was the dealer to sell it? I had to have it. It would be perfect to display a collection. Forget the fact that I didn't have a collection. After I used my stellar negotiating skills, the cupboard was mine. My mom and sister were laughing because they knew I wouldn't make it out of there without buying something big.

There was one small detail I overlooked. Would it fit in the car? At the time, we had my mom's Volvo wagon. No problem. It would be fine. Or would it? We pulled the car up and jammed that big cupboard in the back of the Volvo. It fit perfectly. It took every ounce of cargo area in that car. Oops—where are we going to sit? Mom driving, me in the passenger seat, and thank goodness my sister is skinny. She climbed on top of that big cupboard on her stomach and rode the whole way home (two and a half hours) without a single complaint. After we got home, she told my mom, "Amy has dragged a lot of stuff around for me, and I wasn't going to let her down."

Our bond, our memories, our story.

The cupboard

Patti recovering after a day at the flea market.

The air conditioner cooling off Amy.

OH, DEAR! HOW CAN THIS BE?

On another occasion, we invited Patti to join us on a July trip to the flea market in Brimfield, Massachusetts. Let me remind you that there is nothing hotter than an outdoor flea market in July. Now Amy and I were fast learners, and we had figured out from previous trips to Brimfield that it would be worth it to splurge on a motel room with a pool, which we did. All day long, as we baked in the sunny fields, the only thing that kept us going was thinking about the motel with the wonderfully cool pool water. Finally, it was time to call it a day, and we drove to our motel with much anticipation. We fantasized about how wonderful the pool would feel on our steaming bodies. As soon as we arrived, we threw on our bathing suits as fast as we could, and we were off to indulge ourselves. Oh, dear! Oh, dear! Why was the pool full of about twenty little girls? To our sorrow and dismay, we found the pool had been rented for the afternoon for a birthday party. So much for planning ahead to make our trip a more pleasant one. Instead, we took turns sitting in front of the air-conditioner.

IT'S IN THE DETAILS

My mom is good at this. Making your home speak to you as well as visitors comes from the heart. I recently moved (again) and started with a blank canvas. I love that. (By the way I got the Realtor to give me a discount on his fee if I would stage some of his houses for him.) Hey, you never know when you will need a new career.

The opportunities are countless. I still had so much stuff even after cleaning out three years ago. My kids call me a hoarder. I say I am collecting for a rainy day, such as when you buy a new home or when they get their first home or if you have the urge to change the look of your home (which is often). I recently furnished the kids' apartments completely. I did not hear them complain about getting free stuff and nice stuff, I might add.

When I continue to open boxes—yes, there are still unopened boxes—it is like seeing my items for the first time. Everything is a prospect for new life to be showcased in a different light. Pictures, boxes, succulents, jars, lights, decoys, baskets, even the dog's leash has the potential to find a new home. The perfect spot.

So how do you take care of the details? It is all about trial and error. Like I said earlier, my mom is good at that. Sometimes it helps to have someone other than you put the details together. My mom, daughter, sister, and I do that often, and while we each have different styles and taste, it always seems better when we detail together.

The first thing my mom did when she walked into my new home was to start filling a huge cupboard. She started with books. Books on top, books on the bottom, books upright, books sideways, put the books in, take some books out. You get the general idea. It takes time to figure out the perfect or not so perfect combination to make your items pop. To this day, I am still not satisfied with the cupboard and continue to work on it. I find comfort in adding a lot of different styles to my home. Today I would define my home as" modern farmhouse eclectic."

If you love something, you should buy it because you will always find a place for it. When something speaks to me, and my heart skips a beat when I see it, I buy it. It could be from a garage sale, an antique show or shop, a flea market, on a vacation destination, or just something that I have visualized and finally have the means to purchase. Those are the items that have stayed with me the longest and that breathe new life into my home when I move them around. Those are the details that make my house what it is today.

Details make a difference.

Note all the details.

Ship on shelf along with other items that add detail.

DEFINING STYLE

My divorce was final after two long years. I felt like an onion being peeled back one layer at a time as I went through this process. It was agonizing, painful, and raw. I knew I had made the right decision when my ex enlisted my children to help him move my furniture out of the house and onto the driveway for all the world to see. He did this after I told him I was hiring movers to help me. On the bright side, I lost seven pounds that day after moving antiques and furniture to my new house one load at a time. It was freeing and energizing to have a fresh start. I moved all this heavy, dark, primitive furniture to the garage of my new house and sold it in one big lot to an antique dealer. I was done with it.

Again, an example of how our circumstances can impact our decorating. I worked hard on making my new house bright, airy, and cheery. I had hand-scraped floors, and my father and I hung black-and-white floral wallpaper in the kitchen, which picked up the reflection of the new black, polished granite countertops. He did wainscot around the breakfast benches as well and transformed my kitchen into a happy place for me to spend time, even though I hated to cook.

My newly wallpapered kitchen with wainscoting surrounding the breakfast nook.

My newest decorating style—light, airy, and open
(notice all the details and artwork)

White slip-covered sofas, which are now in my mom's sunroom, over a neutral jute rug
(See? I told you we shop at each other's houses. As you can see, I
was moving on. My accent color in this house was jade green.)

The screened porch morphed into a sunroom.
(more details)

My father built a beautiful sunroom where we spent most of our days. (It was supposed to be a screened porch, but it morphed into an enclosed sunroom.) The windows looked out onto the backyard and a creek.

I also painted the bedroom sour gold and green. It was a warm color against the expanse of the large room. It had bookcases that I filled with items important to me. It was a wonderful getaway and a complete change that reflected my new lifestyle—a single mom with two kids.

Amy's large, open bedroom.
(The chest next to the bed belonged to Patti. Once again, we shopped at each other's houses.)

© CENRIS, Inc.

My house after my divorce.

THE MEN

Ok, so we need to give credit where credit is due. The men in our lives like to work with their hands, thank goodness, and they find satisfaction as well when they complete a job.

From as long as I can remember, my dad was working on a project. One such example was the haunted house on West Avenue in Fairport, New York. That was what my friends called it when we moved in. I was in sixth grade, and to be known as the girl who lived in the haunted house was less than appealing to me. It was an old, dark gray, crusty Victorian from the 1800s. Good thing my parents had a vision, because at the time, I wasn't seeing it. It had a damp, dank, stone-walled, dirt floor cellar that I was sure held the remains of dead bodies. In that basement was a fruit cellar, and I remember finding an old glass jar with the word *King* embossed on the side. That might have been the first time I experienced a treasure hunt.

I recall on Saturdays we would go to that old house and rip up layer after layer of old linoleum to reveal beautiful, wide-plank floors. That was what my mom and I did. Patti, on the other hand, refused to help and wrote a petition on a piece of flooring that said, "This wood is part of the garage, and we don't like to get our hands dirty, so we are signing this petition—signed Patti Kutner, Amy Kutner, and Heidi (our dog)."

The haunted house.

The petition.

Undaunted by Patti's petition, my dad pulled the broken, curving staircase out and built a new one straight to the second floor. The bathrooms were rusty cauldrons for bugs and critters at large. The home had a great garage/barn where my sister and I created a fort. I remember rearranging the old stuff the prior owner left to make tables and places to sit. One time, my sister and I took our wagon down the street so that we could haul an old table out of someone's garbage for our fort. The heavy, dark beams reached high to the ceiling (something I would love today), and when the sun shone through, you could see the dust in the shimmery reflection in the air. We built floats for homecoming in that barn, and my father helped us create a popcorn-shooting tank one year that, of course, won first place. My sister dared me once to jump out of the opening on the front of the barn, and of course I did it and almost broke my neck. We called that our space. I once found an Indian head penny in that old barn.

The house had beautiful, big rooms, and my dad put his heart and soul into that house at the direction of my mom, until it was a work of art. It ended up being featured in the *Democrat and Chronicle* newspaper in Rochester, New York, and it was also on the house tour sponsored by the Fairport Historical Society, 1972.

My dad worked on many other projects, such as renovating two mouse-infested Adirondack homes. My dad has a keen sense of balance and formation. He is an engineer and can fix anything. Why buy new things when you can spend countless hours fixing old things? He can look at something and know whether the placement is going to work without touching a thing. My dad would stare at a potential project, planning for days before embarking on it. My mom and I would think he was dawdling. We would say, "Just get it done," and it would get done, and it would be perfect. Perfect is something my mother and I do not know about. We use more of a trial-and-error approach. My dad was also generous with his time and talent for us girls, as he built us both sunrooms as additions to our homes. My sunroom started as a screened-in porch and morphed into a full-blown sun-infused room with wainscot, high, beamed ceilings enclosed with eight windows. Patti's upgrade included custom bookcases lining the lower half of the walls under the windows in her new den. My dad, over the years, spent countless hours placating mainly Mom with all the project ideas and thoughts she had around making our homes more inviting.

Mark came into my life in 2009. Our children, Connor, and Alex were best friends at the time. Before I knew Mark, I recall a day when the boys were over at my house (I was newly divorced at the time), and they turned to me and said, "If you marry Alex's dad, we will be brothers." The kids were about twelve at the time. Now they are twenty-seven years old and still best friends, and yes, their wish came true—Mark and I are together.

Anyway, when I first met Mark, he asked me if I wanted to go to a financial aid session to learn more about college financing. Now that is the first. Who takes a date to a financial aid fair? I kid him to this day about that date. Mark has an engineering mind and mechanical capability like my dad. He is creative, smart, and downright funny when he wants to be. I am sure he didn't know what he was getting into when he met me. When we first started dating, I would subtly ask if he could fix this or move that or help me mulch the garden or sandblast a table or build a shelf—or better yet build a table. I think you get where I am going here.

In 2016, we built a townhouse, and I had big plans for that place. I really wanted a sliding barn door for my office, and Mark secretly started assembling the most beautiful sliding barn door for me. He wrapped it all up and put a big bow on it and gave it to me for Christmas. I absolutely loved that door. It was perfect.

Amy's dream kitchen

IBlue accent wall in our villa
(My style is still evolving.)

Another time, I said we needed a table for our patio and that reclaimed wood would be great. So out we went, and he built me a fantastic, reclaimed wood table with pipe legs for our patio. Mark's biggest endeavor was refinishing our basement to perfection, with large, red sliding barn doors, a multilayered lacquered bar, a big bedroom, and fantastic storage shelving. Mark does impeccable work, and my dad would often say Mark was doing a good job. This was a high compliment coming from the man who all his life went by the motto "a job worth doing is a job worth doing well."

While living in that house, which was a villa, we acquired a dog. Long story short, we moved again because it was too much to have to walk the dog at 5:00 a.m. in the ice and snow and then late at night after working all day. Call it being lazy. I call it smart because we have an invisible fence. In this new house, the former owner had a first-floor workshop that Mark transformed into a beautiful family room. He added additional windows for a magnificent view of the lake, built a cupboard around the circuit box, built bookshelves on the top of the wall, built shelves underneath with doors, and to top it all off, laid a hardwood floor that sets off the whole room.

Bennie.

The room Mark converted from a shop to a family room.

A bank of cupboards and a bar, built into our kitchen by, of course, my husband.

Milan's carefully crafted molding throughout all our house, with some seasonal decorating added.

Truly we need to give credit where credit is due to these remarkable men who have been such a part of our journey.

Mark, creative and innovative.

Milan, super carpenter, designer, and decorator.

THINGS WE LOVE

AMY'S BEDROOM

Giddy defined as making someone feel excited to the point of disorientation. That is how I feel when I look at my newly updated master bedroom. A smile blazes across my face when I enter the room, and I want to stay in there all day. The large botanical print wallpaper jumps off the walls as if to say, "Here I am! Don't you love me?" The muted shades of blue give a glorious contrast to the stark white walls. Upon the bed, a lush French blue velvet throw gives the room depth and sophistication. (Not to mention it is as soft as an early snowfall in winter.) Blue and white chinoiserie adorn a primitive, tall cabinet, adding pops of color and texture to the room. The myriad shapes and sizes create interest and draw the eye upward. The newly installed hand-scraped hardwoods add something primitive to the room. The stark contrast of polished sophistication and utilitarian simplicity creates curiosity in space. Navy and white swivel chairs invite those who enter to enjoy a bay of windows offering glimpses of the hills and lake. The views at times resemble a painting, especially in fall when the golds and reds of the hillside blend to form a wash of color, hinting at a change in seasons. Handsome antique tiger maple stands embrace the bed with their whimsical blue and white motif. The touch of gold on their rims pays homage to the large, antique, lemon gold gilt mirror across the room. Light bounces off the mirror, creating a sentiment of depth and brightness in the room. A large, floral blue and white floor covering ties the room together, offering a cushion of softness under the foot. Now I don't normally describe my decorating this way, but the room does feel like a poem to me. It is how your house should make you feel, and it is why I love this journey.

Amy's bedroom with a pleasing combination of patterns

Balance of old and new
The sweater Connor wore when he was baptized is
also framed and hung as a focal point.

Christening dress worn by Amy, Patti, and Grace
becomes a decorative part of the bedroom

BARB'S BEDROOM

As you can tell from reading her bedroom story, Amy is a free spirit and fun loving and someone who enjoys life and her home. I, on the other hand, am pretty buttoned up and very conservative. Despite our differences, we have in common our love for decorating our homes, and we both love our bedrooms, which are about as different as night and day. While Amy's is bold with a mixture of many patterns, mine is calm and conservative. Both of us use blue. In Amy's room, the color really pops and makes you happy. Blue is a color usually associated with calmness, serenity, peacefulness, and tranquility, which is exactly what my bedroom feels like to me. It's a refuge from my busy days. A place to relax, read, and rest. The walls are painted gray blue with white trim. The palladium window is treated with a pleated shade, while the large window has plantation shutters. At night, I can lie in my bed and enjoy seeing the moon and the stars. The bed is anchored with a navy-blue dust ruffle and navy-blue pillows. (Navy represents stability.) How appropriate for me. The white Matelassé coverlet has a blue and white overshot coverlet at the foot of the bed, giving the room a feeling of age. Surrounding the room is a chair rail built by—who else? My husband. I spent almost a year looking for the perfect wallpaper to put on the wall under the chair rail. It has a large pattern-on-pattern design in a little darker blue than the walls and is a beautiful English wallpaper. The real treasure in the room is the fireplace, a focal point. I can sit in bed and have my morning coffee or enjoy reading at night by the fire. Whenever I walk into this room, I feel secure and that everything is in order. So important for my well-being. I experience an inner peace and am struck by the beauty of space. I will never tire of this decorating journey, as it gives me such enormous pleasure, and I am so happy to be able to share it with my family.

Barb's Williamsburg bedroom

A cozy fireplace in Barb's bedroom

PATTI'S BEDROOM

Patti's bedroom has an entire wall of windows overlooking the lake. When you look out those windows, it's like looking at an oil painting. One morning as Patti was getting out of her bed, she looked out of her window, and there staring at her were several people in a hot-air balloon, traveling over the lake right next to her bedroom window. She waved at them as she quickly grabbed her bathrobe, and they waved back. Her bedroom has built-in drawers so that no other furniture is needed in the room. It has a lake-like feel with soft greens and blues as a color scheme. She would sit on the love seat and read while having a view of the lake.

Patti's built-in cupboards, which save space in the bedroom

Patti's bedroom, with a view of the lake out the side
windows and the deck off the bedroom

We have so many things we love, but we just wanted to mention our bedrooms because we all have worked so hard to create the look, feel, and ambience that we were after as we designed our rooms.

COLLECTIONS

Collections can enhance our homes in many ways. They tell another story about what we love, what our interests are, and maybe where we have been. They can be a focal point for the room, depending on how you display your items. Shelving is a creative way to display a collection, or perhaps place it on the mantel of the fireplace. You want to group them together, so they make a statement and draw an eye toward them. Collections may also reinforce your style. For instance, if your theme is farmhouse country, a collection of baskets, crocks, and cutting boards will create the effect you are trying to maintain. Collections also become items you seek when you are shopping in some of the places we suggested, causing you great joy when you find a new item to add to your collection. Collections can also be a source for learning about history, places, or people, adding to your knowledge of decorating and the world. Shown in the next two pictures are samples of how to display a collection. Also included is information about two collections we wanted to share.

Black-and-white collection tied together by one color

Shorebird collection displayed on shelves built by Milan
Boat painting collection in a grouping makes a statement as well

NANTUCKET LIGHTSHIP
BASKET COLLECTIONS

As we sought items to decorate our homes it was easy to fall in love with special items that turned into collections. One such collection that we were all interested in were Nantucket lightship baskets.

Nantucket is a very special place to our family and has had an influence on the decorating of our homes. It is where Patti and Andy and Mark and Amy both spent their honeymoons. For ten years, we vacationed there as a family, returning on and off over the years since.

Nantucket is a sandbar thirty miles off the coast of Cape Cod, Massachusetts. In the 1800s, it was known as the dominant center of the whaling industry and was a busy, thriving community. In future years, with the decline of the whaling industry, Nantucket faced economic hardship. In the late nineteenth century, outsiders began to discover this hidden gem. Real estate prices soared, and Nantucket's economy blossomed as people flocked to the island.

On a hot August morning, we boarded the ferry for our first trip to Nantucket. There were cars boarding, bikes being wheeled on, babies being pushed in strollers, and all kinds of dogs on leashes. It was very chaotic, but once on board, it was even worse. No place to sit, every seat taken, so people were sitting on the floor, resting against their backpacks. Why would anyone go through this? What was so special about this island?

We soon found out. Nantucket is a very special place. When you walk on the beach or through town and begin to learn about the history of Nantucket, you can't help falling in love with it. The homes are beautiful, from the tiniest to the largest mansions. All the homes have weathered cedar shingles in a soft, warm gray color with white trim. Window boxes are overflowing with beautiful plantings, the harbor is full of impressive yachts and sailboats, and as you walk on the brick streets, you are treated to some of the best shopping anywhere. Restaurants abound with delicious food choices, and the warm sun, the bushy blue hydrangeas, the smell of the salt water, and the gentle breezes are all part of what makes Nantucket.

Soon we became interested in the lightship baskets that you see all over the island.

The history of the Nantucket lightship baskets attracted us because of their simplicity, grace, and elegance. We saw them as a form of folk art. The native American tribe of the Wampanoag Nation on Nantucket was making splint-type baskets very early on, and they were quite different from what we know today as a lightship basket, but they may have served to inspire later basket makers. The baskets evolved over time, and many influences contributed to their design, beginning with these first baskets made by the Native Americans on the island. The use of available materials, construction techniques particular to the island, and the slotted wooden base for the basket also contributed to the design of today's baskets.

The whaling industry in the late eighteenth and nineteenth centuries made Nantucket the capital of the industry, and it was a busy port. Because of the need for barrels to store the whale oil, coopers came to the island and began building barrels or casks, the construction of which influenced local basket makers to change the design of the baskets they were making. The coopers probably had the greatest influence on the design of the basket as we know it today. Another change that took place was caused by the whaling ships that went all over the world. They began bringing rattan back on their return trips, to be used by the weavers in place of the wooden splint baskets that were formally used in prior basket making.

Unfortunately, there was no basket maker on the island, so baskets were being imported from Europe until Jose Reyes came to the island and began making a basket in a new design, called the friendship basket, lighthouse purse. These baskets became popular as gifts and signs of friendship. After their introduction to the island, it became a tradition for every girl who graduated from Nantucket High School to receive one for her graduation. By the 1850s, the rattan lightship basket had been perfected and was being made by islanders, but I'm getting ahead of myself.

Amy's lightship basket purse with carved whale adorning the top.

More of Amy's baskets.

In the mid-1800s, it came to the attention of Congress, via shipmasters who sailed around the waters of Nantucket, that Congress needed to mark some of the shoals along the Nantucket coast that were hazardous to ship navigation. These shoals extended off the coast of Nantucket. The conditions were not suitable for a lighthouse, so it was decided to place a lightship in the area to alert passing ships to stay away from the area where these shoals were located. This area was extremely dangerous, and it took time to build a ship that could withstand the conditions it would be exposed to.

In 1856, the *New South Shoal* ship was launched to warn ships of the danger. The men had duties they had to perform as they spent months at a time out on this ship, but they also had considerable free time, making boredom another hazard of the job. Making baskets from rattan was a fully developed method of basket making, and it gave the men something to do. They would make the baskets as gifts for loved ones or would sell them for anywhere from a dollar fifty to fifty dollars. Today, these baskets start at around $500.

Label on the bottom of Patti's antique lightship basket, authenticating her purchase as a real antique basket.

Patti's antique baskets.

Sometimes you will find a basket with the bottom painted a color. This was done by the owner so that when she took her basket to a potluck supper or some such event, she would be able to identify which basket was hers.

Today, these older baskets have taken their place in museums and are valued as antiques.

I do not own an antique lightship basket, but in the 1990s, while searching at the Elephant Trunk Flea Market in New Milford, Connecticut, I found a set of three nesting baskets and one larger one made by a man named Wayne Martin. I learned that he is a woodworker and basket maker who lives in the South and teaches classes on making Nantucket baskets. I have no idea what I paid for the four baskets, but I'm sure it was under a hundred dollars. I was able to speak to him about his baskets, and he assured me he fell in love with the beauty and simplicity of these baskets the first time he saw one. He has made all his own molds, allowing him to make many baskets, which he offers for sale. While these baskets are not made in Nantucket, I think they are very well made by a craftsman who values and appreciates Nantucket baskets. I enjoy owning them because they are reminders of our time spent on this special island.

My Elephant Trunk Flea Market Nantucket baskets.

COLLECTING BLUE AND WHITE CHINA

MY BLUE AND WHITE COLLECTION

Sometimes a collection will just come to you as a gift, an inheritance, or, as in my case, left in a purchased home. Fortunately for us, the former owners left all the furnishings in the house when they sold it to us. Sorting through the rooms to decide what to keep and what to dispose of allowed us to find some unexpected treasures that we still enjoy today. One was a whole set of Blue Willow dishes. Now I love anything blue. As I learned more about Blue Willow, I was so excited to have found these special dishes. And thus began my interest in collecting more Blue Willow and learning about transfer ware.

The Blue Willow pattern is also referred to as transfer ware, which means the design was etched onto a piece of copper plate and then printed on a thin piece of paper. The paper was applied to the plate and fired. Thus, the design was transferred rather than hand-painted, making the plates much easier to produce and more affordable.

The Blue Willow pattern tells the legend of two ill-fated Chinese lovers. There are several variations of the story, but basically the story remains the same. A beautiful young girl falls in love with her father's clerk. The father disapproves of the marriage, causing them to decide they must elope if they want to be together. They are seen in the lower right-hand corner running across the bridge, with her father in pursuit. Her father, depending on which version you are learning about, chases after them with the intent of killing them. Depending on which version you are reading, they either jump to their deaths or the father kills them. You then see them at the top of the plate, returning as two lovebirds.

The basic elements of the pattern are a footbridge with three people, a boat, a willow tree, and the two lovebirds. Also, flowers, apple trees, and a garden fence are usually found in the pattern. For some folks, collecting the various stories is as much a part of the fun as collecting the dishes. When you compare the story to the dishes, they become even more real, and it's hard not to believe the legend. Also, you should know that the Blue Willow legends were not created until after the Blue Willow pattern in China became popular. The stories were invented by English and Americans, and the pattern was designed by the English and not the Chinese.

Blue Willow became popular not only in England but also in the United States. As the pioneers traveled across the country, they brought with them sets of Blue Willow ware or ordered them from England. Blue and white were the most popular colors for dishes in the nineteenth century. If you watch old pioneer movies, you will often see this pattern appearing on dishes in the movie.

Note the lovers running across the bridge in the lower left-hand corner, being chased by the father, and the lovebirds appearing at the top of the plate.

PATTI'S BLUE AND WHITE COLLECTION

Patti, on the other hand, began collecting blue and white Soba Choko cups while she was living in Japan. She had time to visit antique shops and became interested in these cups. She had many of them displayed on a sectioned shelf that her father built her as a Christmas present. (Once again, he used his skills to contribute to our decorating plans.)

Soba Choko cups were used as spice holders or drinking vessels but later became primarily used to hold sauce for dipping noodles. They were also used for soup and sake. They made a beautiful collection, which she treasured.

Blue and white bowl from Patti's blue and white collection.

Soba Choko cups from Patti's collection.

AMY'S BLUE AND WHITE COLLECTION

Amy's collection began when she moved to her present house, which is decorated with a blue and white color scheme. She has found all kinds of blue and white porcelain pieces in antique shops, the Restore, TJ Maxx, Marshall's, and gift shops and has used them to enhance her decorating. Since her house has very tall ceilings, she has bought some large pieces, which have a dramatic effect on her house. Each piece contributes to the beauty of her home.

Among the three of us, we have many other items we love and treasure, but we mentioned these two to give you, the reader, an idea of how collections come to be, how they influence our lives and our decorating, and what we can learn from having them. Think about what you might like to collect that would reflect what you love and what you would enjoy learning more about, and then begin collecting those items. We hope you have as much fun decorating your home with items you love as we have had.

OUR STORY NEVER ENDS

We talked at the beginning of this book about how our homes make us happy—how this is a journey, a story that never ends, but it did for one of us. My mom and I, as mentioned before, are dedicating this book to my sister, who at a young age was taken from us, too soon. My mom and I continue the journey along with the addition of my daughter, Grace. I know my sister would love to hear that Grace has joined us in our decorating searches. We continue to scour antique shops, decorating magazines, do-it-yourself guides, home stores, and all the other places we have mentioned to seek out the next best purchase for our homes. The thrill remains at creating something beautiful, be it a table setting, flower arrangement, group of paintings, or a tiny collection. Nothing remains the same in our homes as we go from season to season in anticipation of the next metamorphosis of our homes, except the consistent thought of my sister reminding us that "less is more, and space is good." She was a perfectionist with impeccable taste. She is always with us in spirit, and as we embark on our buying adventures, we are reminded that life is short and that you should buy what makes you happy.

Mom, Patti, and me.

Printed in the United States
by Baker & Taylor Publisher Services